KHALID

by Emily Hudd

Raintree is an imprint of Capstone Global Library Limited, a company incorporated in England and Wales having its registered office at 264 Banbury Road, Oxford, OX2 ?DY – Registered company number: 6695582

www.raintree.co.uk
myorders@raintree.co.uk

Text © Capstone Global Library Limited 2020
The moral rights of the proprietor have been asserted.

All rights reserved. No part of this publication may be reproduced in any form or by any means (including photocopying or storing it in any medium by electronic means and whether or not transiently or incidentally to some other use of this publication) without the written permission of the copyright owner, except in accordance with the provisions of the Copyright, Designs and Patents Act 1988 or under the terms of a licence issued by the Copyright Licensing Agency, Barnard's Inn, 86 Fetter Lane, London, EC4A 1 EN (www.cla.co.uk). Applications for the copyright owner's written permission should be addressed to the publisher.

Edited by Claire Vanden Branden
Designed by Becky Daum
Original illustrations © Capstone Global Library Limited 2020
Production by Melissa Martin
Originated by Capstone Global Library Limited
Printed and bound in India. PO 864

ISBN 978 1 4747 8744 4

British Library Cataloguing in Publication Data
A full catalogue record for this book is available from the British Library

Acknowledgements
Alamy: Daniel DeSlover/ZUMA Press, Inc./Alamy Live News, 10–11; Kim M. Leland/Gonzales Photo/Alamy Live News, 16–17; Samy Khabthani/Gonzales Photo, 26–27; AP Images: Jordan Strauss/Invision, cover; Newscom: PG/Splash News, 22; Rex Features: 21, Steven Ferdman, 15; Shutterstock Images: agwilson, 25, Ben Houdijk, 5, 28, Kathy Hutchins, 7, 13, 18–19, 31, leoks/Shutterstock Images, 9
Design Elements: Shutterstock Images

Every effort has been made to contact copyright holders of material reproduced in this book. Any omissions will be rectified in subsequent printings if notice is given to the publisher.

All the internet addresses (URLs) given in this book were valid at the time of going to press. However, due to the dynamic nature of the internet, some addresses may have changed, or sites may have changed or ceased to exist since publication. While the author and publisher regret any inconvenience this may cause readers, no responsibility for any such changes can be accepted by either the author or the publisher.

CONTENTS

CHAPTER ONE
A NEW STAR 4

CHAPTER TWO
EARLY LIFE 8

CHAPTER THREE
RISE TO FAME 14

CHAPTER FOUR
MAKING IT BIG 20

Glossary 28
Timeline 29
Activity 30
Find out more 32
Index 32

CHAPTER 1

A NEW Star

Fans waited with excitement. Then they started to scream. Khalid was walking on stage. He began to sing his song "American Teen". He pointed at them and smiled. People sang along.

Khalid was on his first music **tour**. It lasted from July to September 2017. Khalid travelled across the United States. He had 25 shows. The tour was for his first **album**, *American Teen*. It had come out earlier that year.

Khalid enjoys dancing during his performances.

THE GRAMMYS

Khalid was **nominated** five times for the 60th **Grammy Awards**. One was for Song of the Year. Khalid worked with the artist Logic. They made the song "1-800-273-8255". The song's name is the phone number for the US national suicide prevention helpline. The song was about people who deal with hard times. It was hugely popular.

Khalid's music journey had just started. In 2016 he was a school student. By 2017 he was a famous singer.

Khalid did not win a Grammy Award in 2018, but he has won many awards since then.

CHAPTER 2

EARLY Life

Khalid Robinson was born on 11 February 1998 in Fort Stewart, Georgia, USA. His father died when Khalid was young. His mother was in the **army**. Khalid moved a lot as a child. He lived in Germany for six years. He also spent four years living in New York.

Khalid became interested in music when he was three years old. His mother sang around the house. His family listened to music a lot while he was growing up.

Khalid lived in Heidelberg, Germany, for a while when he was young.

Khalid's music has been inspired by his experiences growing up.

THE MOVE

In 2015 Khalid and his family moved to El Paso, Texas. He was 17 years old. It was not easy to move. He missed his friends in New York. He wrote music to help him feel better.

Khalid spent his spare time recording songs. He later said that moving to Texas turned out well for him. He met new people and he had new song ideas.

Khalid took his emotions and turned them into song lyrics.

CHAPTER 3

RISE TO Fame

In 2016, while Khalid was still at school, he started posting songs on SoundCloud. SoundCloud is a music sharing website.

His music spread. People loved it.

Then Khalid went to a recording studio.

He made the song "Location".

Khalid thought he would grow up to be a music teacher before he became famous.

People listened to "Location" on their phones. They shared it with friends. Khalid left school in May 2016. That same day, television star Kylie Jenner listened to the song. She posted about it on her social media. Then the song became very popular. Khalid's life changed forever.

"LOCATION"

"Location" has nearly half a million views on YouTube. It has been listened to nearly 100 million times on SoundCloud.

Khalid soon began singing in front of thousands of people.

Khalid is inspired by many different kinds of music.

FIRST ALBUM

The music company RCA Records saw Khalid's talent. They helped him make his album, *American Teen*. It came out on 3 March 2017. It sold more than 1 million copies.

CHAPTER 4

MAKING It Big

Many people started to notice Khalid. They wanted to work with him. He was young and fresh and he could sing many types of music.

Khalid sang with Shawn Mendes at the 2018 **Billboard Music Awards**.

"THE WAYS"

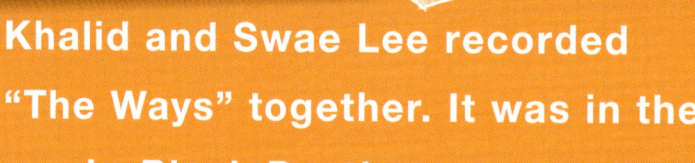

Khalid and Swae Lee recorded "The Ways" together. It was in the movie *Black Panther*.

WORKING WITH OTHER ARTISTS

Khalid worked with many artists in 2018. He sang with rapper Kendrick Lamar. He worked with young artists like Shawn Mendes. Some of his songs were in films.

Khalid also worked with singer Normani. They made the song "Love Lies". It came out in February 2018. It has been listened to millions of times on Spotify. It was also in the film *Love, Simon*.

SECOND ALBUM

Khalid made his second album in 2018. It was called *Suncity*. It had seven songs. One is in Spanish. *Suncity* was Billboard's top **R&B** album in November 2018.

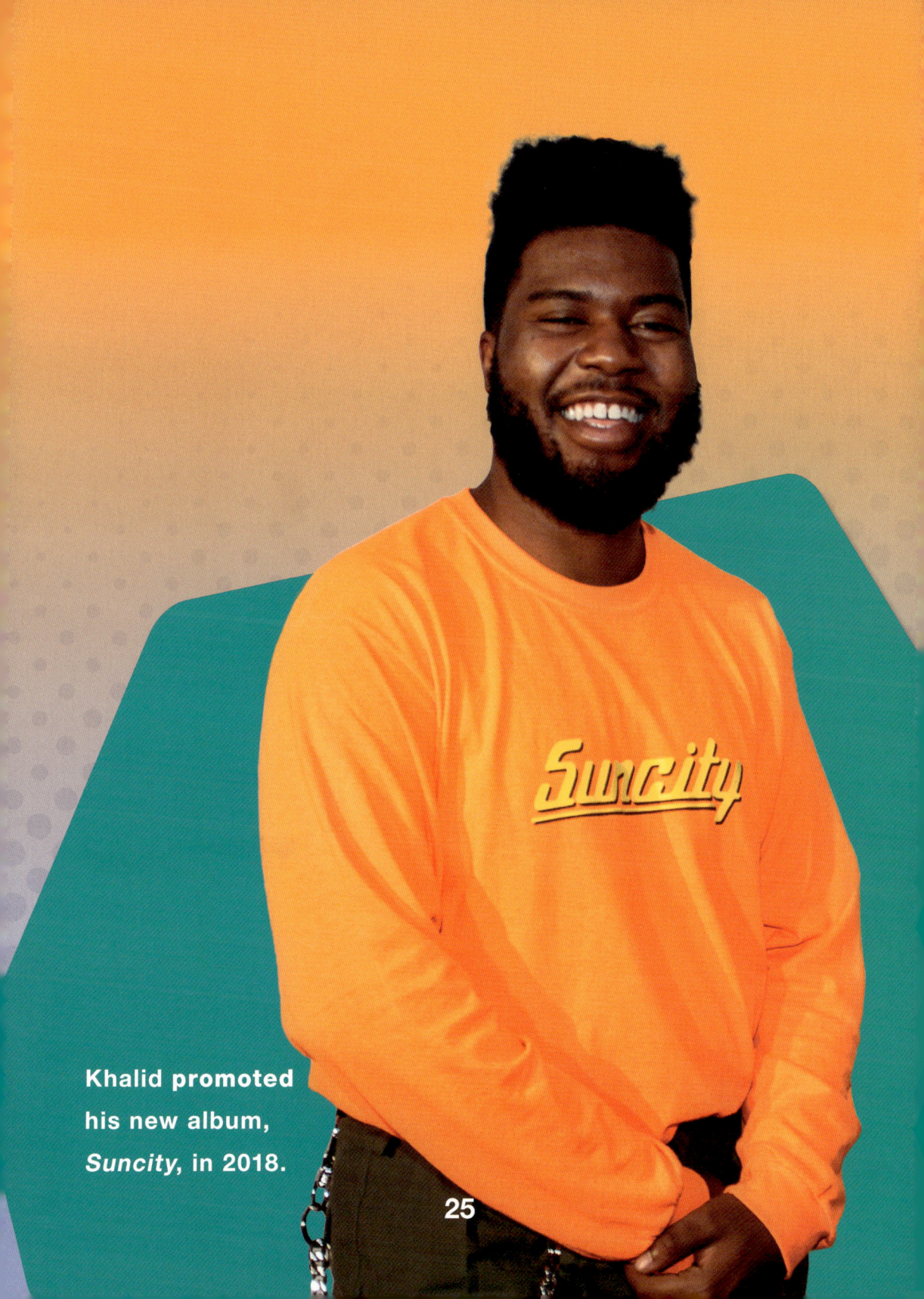

Khalid promoted his new album, *Suncity*, in 2018.

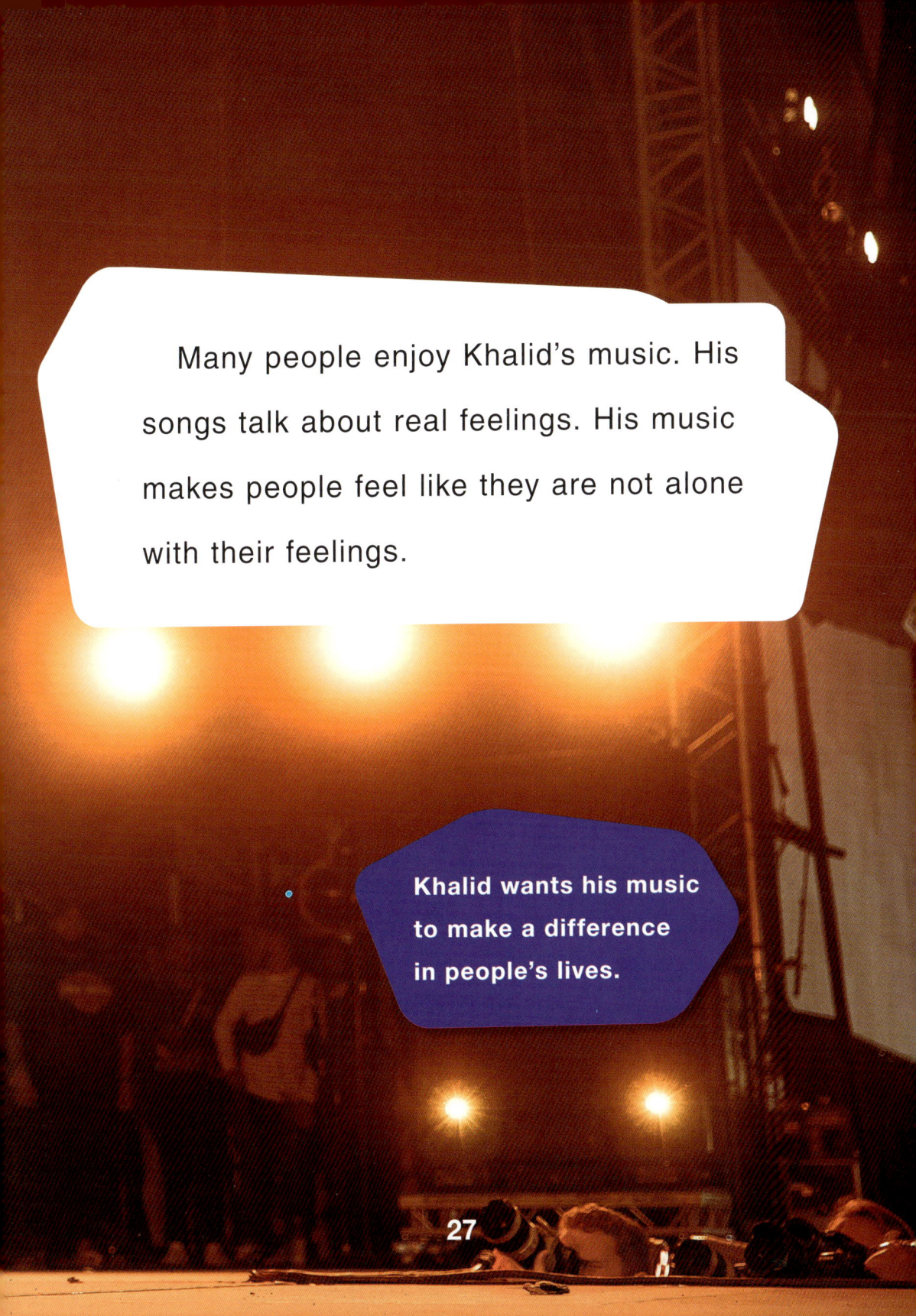

Many people enjoy Khalid's music. His songs talk about real feelings. His music makes people feel like they are not alone with their feelings.

Khalid wants his music to make a difference in people's lives.

GLOSSARY

album
a collection of songs

Billboard
a music company that ranks songs and artists

Grammy Award
an award that honours the best artists in music

military
part of the United States armed forces

nominate
to suggest that a person might be the right one for a job or an award

promote
to try and encourage sales of something

R&B
(short for rhythm and blues) popular music usually including parts of blues and African-American folk music and marked by a strong beat and simple chords

TIMELINE

1998: Khalid Robinson is born on 11 February.

2015: Khalid moves to El Paso, Texas.

2016: Khalid leaves school. On the same day, Kylie Jenner puts "Location" on her Snapchat feed.

2017: Khalid releases his first album, *American Teen*.

2017: Khalid goes on tour.

2017: Khalid is nominated for five Grammys.

2018: Khalid makes his second album, *Suncity*.

ACTIVITY

WRITE YOUR OWN SONG

Khalid writes about things that happen in his life. He takes his feelings and turns them into music. Take a few minutes to think about something big that has happened in your life. How did it make you feel? Write down your experience. Now turn those feelings into a song! Don't forget to give your song a title.

FIND OUT MORE

Feel inspired to learn more about music? Check out these resources:

Books

Create Your Own Music (Media Genius), Matthew Anniss (Raintree, 2017)

Recording and Promoting Your Music (I'm in the Band), Matthew Anniss (Raintree, 2014)

You Can Work in Music (You Can Work in the Arts), Carolina Walker (Raintree, 2019)

Website

DK Find Out!: World Music Day
www.dkfindout.com/us/more-find-out/special-events/world-music-day

INDEX

"1-800-273-8255" 6
American Teen 5, 19
Black Panther 22
El Paso, Texas 11
Grammy Awards 6
Jenner, Kylie 16
Lamar, Kendrick 23
"Location" 15–16
Love, Simon 23
Mendes, Shawn 23
New York 8, 11
Normani 23
RCA Records 19
SoundCloud 14, 16
Spotify 23
Suncity 24
tour 5